The Wild Life of PENGUINS

By Camilla de la Bédoyère

WINDMILL BOOKS

THE WILD SIDE

Published in 2015 by **WINDMILL BOOKS**, an Imprint of Rosen Publishing
29 East 21st Street, New York, NY 10010

Publishing Director: Belinda Gallagher
Creative Director: Jo Cowan
Editorial Director: Rosie Neave
Senior Editor: Sarah Parkin
Designer: Jo Cowan
Image Manager: Liberty Newton
Production Manager: Elizabeth Collins
Reprographics: Stephan Davis, Jennifer Cozens, Thom Allaway, Anthony Cambray, Lorraine King

ACKNOWLEDGEMENTS

The publishers would like to thank Mike Foster (Maltings Partnership), Joe Jones, and Richard Watson (Bright Agency) for the illustrations they contributed to this book. All other artwork from the Miles Kelly Artwork Bank.

The publishers would like to thank the following sources for the use of their photographs: t = top, b = bottom, l = left, r = right, c = center, bg = background, rt = repeated throughout. **Cover** (front) David Tipling/Nature Picture Library, (back) niall dunne/Shutterstock; (Speech panel) Tropinina Olga. **Ardea** 15(t) D. Parer & E. Parer-Cook. **Corbis** 6 Tim Davis; 7(t) Frans Lanting, (b) Yva Momatiuk & John Eastcott/Minden Pictures; 10 Tim Davis; 11(t) Andy Rouse; 15(b) Michael S. Nolan/ Robert Harding Specialist Stock; 20 Wayne Lynch/All Canada Photos; 21(b) Frans Lanting. **Nature Picture Library** 1 David Tipling; 11(b) David Tipling. **Photo Discs/Digital Stock** Heading bar (rt). **Shutterstock** Joke panel (rt) Tropinina Olga; Learn a Word panel (rt) donatas1205; Learn a Word cartoon Nelia Sapronova; 2 Palo_ok; 3 Moritz Buchty; 4–5 Eric Isselée; 5(bl) Jordan Tan, (r) Jan Martin Will; 8–9(bg) Lucy Baldwin; 8 & 9(heading bar & panel b) buruhtan; 8(penguin panel tr) Joney, (brush stroke tl) Ambient Ideas, (speech bubble br) tachyglossus; 9(panel tr) april70; 12–13 lfstewart; 13(tr) Karel Gallas; 14 Mogens Trolle; 16–17(bg) llaszlo; 16(heading bar) bruniewska, (panel tr) andrewshka, (penguins cl) Memo Angeles; 17(panel tl) donatas1205, (panel tr) pichayasri, (heading panel b) Veerachai Viteeman, (panel b) samiah samin, (brush stroke b) Ambient Ideas; 18 AndreAnita; 19(t) Anders Peter Photography, (b) steve estvanik; 21(t) Mogens Trolle.

LIBRARY OF CONGRESS CATALOGING-IN-PUBLICATION DATA

De la Bédoyère, Camilla, author.
 The wild life of penguins / Camilla de la Bedoyere.
    pages cm. — (The wild side)
 Includes index.
 ISBN 978-1-4777-5503-7 (pbk.)
 ISBN 978-1-4777-5504-4 (6 pack)
 ISBN 978-1-4777-5502-0 (library binding)
1. Penguins—Juvenile literature. I. Title.
 QL696.S473D452 2015
 598.47—dc23
 598.47—dc23

                        2014027098

Manufactured in the United States of America

CPSIA Compliance Information: Batch #CW15WM: For Further Information contact Rosen Publishing, New York, New York at 1-800-237-9932

Contents

What are you?

I am a penguin!

I am a bird, but I cannot fly. I spend most of my life in the sea.

Waterproof feathers

Humboldt penguin

Flippers

Webbed feet

Q. Why do penguins carry fish in their beaks?

A. Because they haven't got any pockets!

Strong beak

White chest

Penguin family

There are 17 types of penguins. These seabirds stand upright and have short legs.

Emperor penguin
45 inches (114.3 cm) tall

Little penguin
14 inches (35.5 cm) tall

I am a speedy swimmer!

My wings are more like flippers. They help me to "fly" through the water. My body is streamlined.

King penguins

Walking on ice

Penguins waddle when they walk. Sometimes they slide on the snow and ice on their fronts.

Q. What goes black, white, black, white, black, white?

A. A penguin rolling down a hill!

Emperor penguins

Bouncy!

Rockhopper penguins hop from rock to rock by the sea.

Activity time

Get ready to make and do!

Penguin hunt

Look in books and on the Internet to try and find the names of all 17 types of penguins. Then look at pictures and draw your favorites.

Draw me!

YOU WILL NEED:
pencils · paper

1. Draw two squashed circles for the penguin's head and body.

2. Add the eye, beak, neck, flipper, tail, and feet.

3. Draw the penguin's chest. Now shape the tail and feet.

Now color me in and give me a name!

Little friends

Ask for help!

YOU WILL NEED:
colored felt · scissors
toilet paper tube
glue · markers

HERE'S HOW:
1. Cut felt shapes for the penguin's eyes, beak, belly, flippers and feet.
2. Cover the toilet paper tube with black felt and glue it down.
3. Glue the felt pieces into place.
4. Draw on extra details, such as the eyes.

Penguin cookies

YOU WILL NEED:
packet of plain, round cookies
icing pens in different colors
or colored royal icing

HERE'S HOW:
1. Use black icing to color in the top of the cookie. Allow to dry.
2. Fill in the rest of the cookie with white icing. Allow to dry.
3. Use other colors to add eyes, a beak and feet to your cookie.

Now make lots of penguins so you have a whole colony to play with!

What are your babies called?

My babies are called chicks.

The female lays one egg and we both look after it. We rest the egg on our feet so it does not get cold. Our chick is growing inside it.

King penguin parents

Egg

Fluffy feathers

Penguin chicks have thick, fluffy feathers called down. Down helps them to stay warm.

Q. What is a baby penguin's favorite game?

A. Slide-and-seek!

Chilly chicks

When it snows chicks can get chilly. They huddle together in groups for warmth.

Emperor penguin chicks

Where do you live?

Gentoo penguins

I live in cold places!

Most penguins live near the South Pole, where it is very cold. There are lots of fish in the sea, so it is a good place to live.

Warm water

Some penguins like to be warm. African penguins live on beaches around South Africa.

Q. What do you call a penguin in a desert?

A. Lost!

What do you eat?

I eat fish.

My chick is too young to swim, so I catch a fish and feed it to him.

Gentoo penguins

Catching fish

Penguins catch fish in their beaks, which have sharp edges and hooks on the end.

Galapagos penguins

Q. Where do penguins go swimming?

A. At the South Pool!

Spiky tongues

Penguins have little spikes on their tongues. The spikes grip onto wriggling fish to stop them escaping.

Puzzle time

Can you solve all the puzzles?

Lucky catch

Which lucky penguin caught a fish? Trace the lines with your finger to find out.

Pippa

Percy

Polly

True or false?

1. Penguins are birds.
2. Penguin babies are called kittens.
3. Thick, fluffy feathers are called down.

Find the penguin

Starting with the letter in the middle of the circles, follow the letters in the wheels to find the names of three penguins.

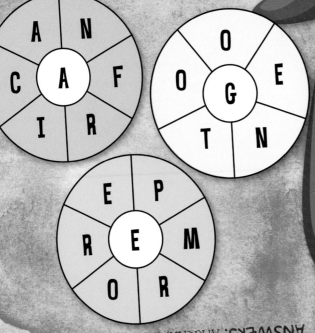

ANSWERS: AFRICAN, GENTOO, EMPEROR

Odd one out

Only one of these birds can fly. Do you know which one?

Penguin

Ostrich

Emu

Duck

Kiwi

ANSWER: Duck

Who's who?

A   B   C

Use these clues to match each penguin to its name.

1. **Chinstrap penguins** have black stripes under their chins.

2. **African penguins** have black and white faces.

3. **Macaroni penguins** have yellow crests.

ANSWER: 1. Chinstrap – B 2. African – C 3. Macaroni – A

I am colorful!

All penguins have black and white feathers, but some of us have yellow, red, or orange feathers too. I have a yellow crest (head feathers).

Royal penguin

Q. What is black and white, and red all over?
A. A shy penguin!

18

Yellow eyes

Shy birds that live in New Zealand, yellow-eyed penguins are now very rare.

LEARN A WORD:

rare

When there are very few alive in the wild and they are uncommon.

Black faces

Adélie penguins have black faces. Males and females look the same.

Do you live together?

Yes, we live in big groups!

A group of penguins is called a colony. We make our nests in one place. Living together helps us to stay warm and safe.

Gentoo penguins

Show off!

Male penguins stretch up tall, point their beaks upwards, beat their flippers and call loudly to impress females.

Chinstrap penguin

Q. What is black and white and has eight wheels?

A. A penguin on roller skates!

Fight time

Penguins sometimes fight with each other. They call loudly and flap their flippers.

King penguins

Poppy goes on vacation

Poppy the penguin didn't like snow. She lived near the South Pole in Antarctica, where there is snow everywhere.

One day, the other penguins gave Poppy a plane, a map, and a mobile phone. They said she should go somewhere warm and have a vacation.

Poppy looked at the map and decided she would go to Africa. She said goodbye to her friends and flew off in her plane.

When Poppy got to Africa she went to the seaside and read her book in the sunshine. She ate lots of ice cream,

but it didn't taste as nice as fish. Poppy sent a text to her friends: I am too hot and I don't like ice cream.

They replied: Go for a swim and find some fish to eat!

Poppy got back in her plane and flew to a river. She jumped into the water. It was lovely and cool, and there were lots of fish to eat.

But there was something else in the river too – a crocodile! Snap, snap went the crocodile's jaws as it chased Poppy. She jumped out of the river and took a photo of the crocodile with her phone. She sent it to her friends with another message: I don't like crocodiles!

They replied: Go to the North Pole. There are no crocodiles there!

So Poppy flew her plane to the North Pole. She stepped out of the plane and dived into the icy water, where she found lots of fish.

She sent a text to her friends: This is just like home. I like it here!

And they replied: Watch out for polar bears!

Poppy looked around and saw a huge white bear running towards her. She jumped into her plane and, as she flew back to the South Pole, Poppy thought that there is no place like home!

By Camilla de la Bédoyère

Glossary

beak a part of the mouth that sticks out on some animals and is used to tear food

colony a group of penguins

crest a showy growth on the head of an animal

down fluffy feathers that form the first covering of a young bird, or a lower layer for adult birds

flap to move up and down or back and forth

flipper a wide, flat "arm" used for swimming

spiky having many pointy pieces or sections

waddle walk with short steps and a clumsy side-to-side motion

waterproof able to keep water out

webbed connected by skin

Websites

For web resources related to the subject of this book, go to:
www.windmillbooks.com/weblinks
and select this book's title.

Index